THE WORLD OCEAN

Anita Ganeri & Josy Bloggs

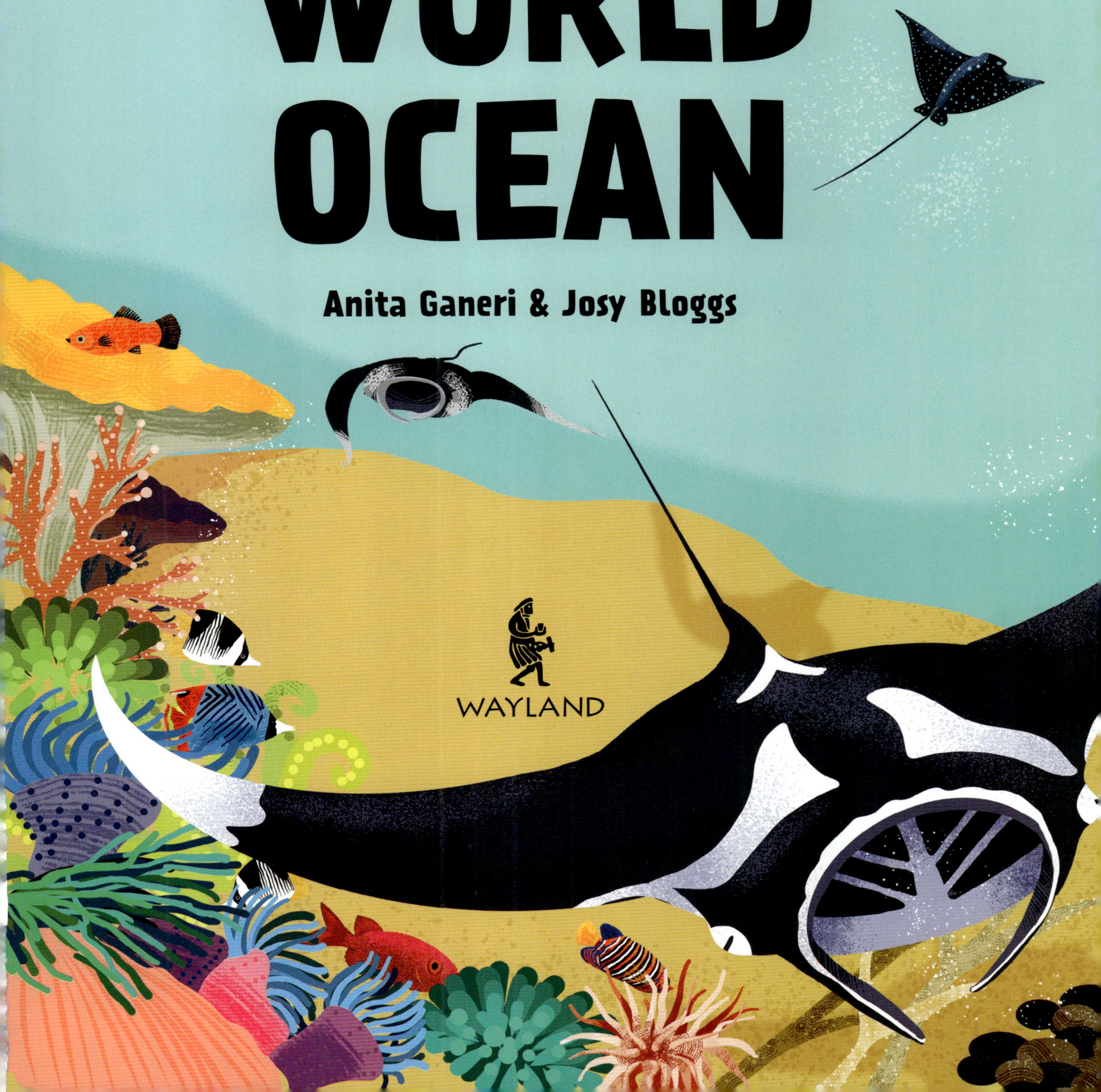

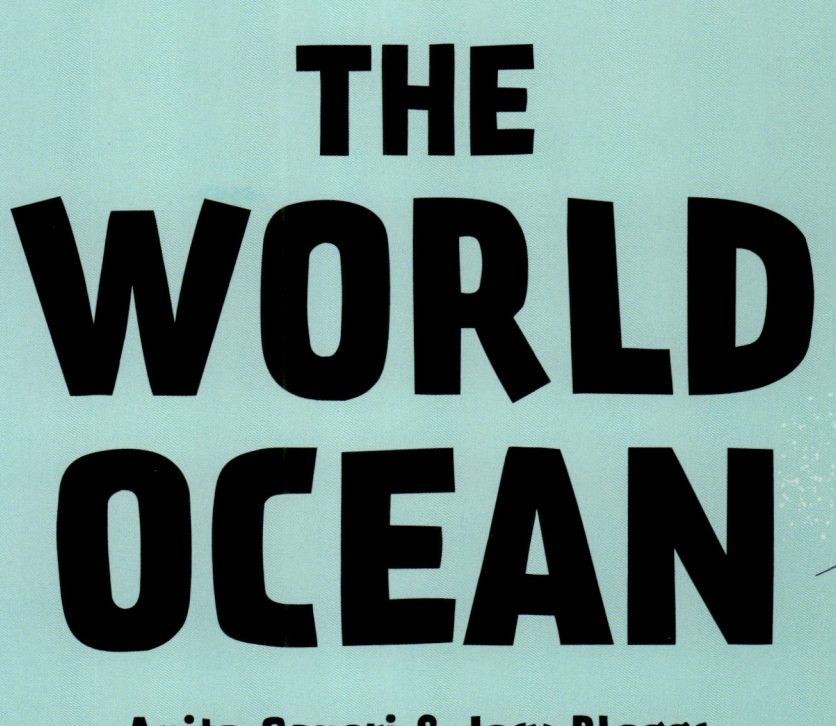

WAYLAND

Contents

A world of water 4

Chapter 1: Around the oceans
The Arctic Ocean 6
The Atlantic Ocean 8
The Indian Ocean 10
The Pacific Ocean 12
The Southern Ocean 14

Chapter 2: Unique features
Wind, weather and currents 16
Volcanoes and islands 18
The Great Barrier Reef 20
Pacific islands 22
An icy ocean 24
Arctic seasons 26

Chapter 3: Voyages of discovery
Crossing the Atlantic 28
Exploring the Pacific 30
Arctic journeys 32
Indian Ocean explorers 34
Southern science 36

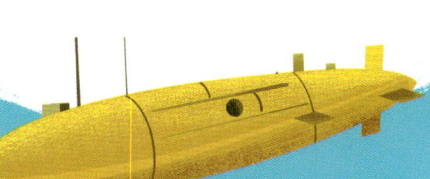

Chapter 4: Ocean wildlife
Life in the Arctic 38
Pacific animals 40
Pacific plants 42
Penguin power 44
Indian Ocean animals 46
Atlantic green turtles 48

Chapter 5: Looking ahead
Indian Ocean riches 50
Indian Ocean in danger 52
Atlantic future 54
The changing Arctic 56
Saving the Southern Ocean 58

The oceans in facts and figures 60
Glossary 62
Index 64

A world of water

If you could view the Earth from space, you would see a planet covered largely by water. More than two-thirds of the Earth's surface lies beneath oceans and seas. This is why it is often called the 'blue planet'.

The largest ocean

The Earth has five oceans: the Pacific, Atlantic, Indian, Arctic and Southern. The Pacific is the largest and deepest of the five. It contains half of all the world's sea water, and, at its widest point, stretches nearly halfway around the world.

ATLANTIC OCEAN

INDIAN OCEAN

SOUTHERN OCEAN

A single ocean

Two hundred million years ago, there was one vast ocean, called Panthalassa, surrounding a giant landmass, called Pangaea. As the plates of the Earth's crust drifted around, Pangaea broke up into today's continents and Panthalassa became the oceans.

Where the water came from

Scientists are still trying to work out where the water in the oceans came from. There are various theories. One is that it may have been part of the rocky material that came together to form the Earth, 4.5 billion years ago.

The oceans and us

The Pacific and other oceans are vitally important for life on Earth. Water from the oceans forms part of the water cycle that brings us fresh water from rain and rivers. Ocean currents help to spread heat around the Earth. The oceans also provide food for millions of people.

Chapter 1: Around the oceans

The Arctic Ocean

The Arctic Ocean is almost entirely surrounded by land. Narrow passages connect it to the Atlantic and Pacific Oceans. It is cold and icy here for much of the year.

At the surface of the Arctic Ocean, the water temperature is about -2°C. This is cold enough for the salty seawater to freeze over, creating a thick layer of sea ice, called pack ice.

Arctic seas

Some parts of the Arctic Ocean are called seas. These are areas of water partly enclosed by islands or peninsulas. They include the Barents, Greenland, Chukchi, Laptev and Norwegian Seas.

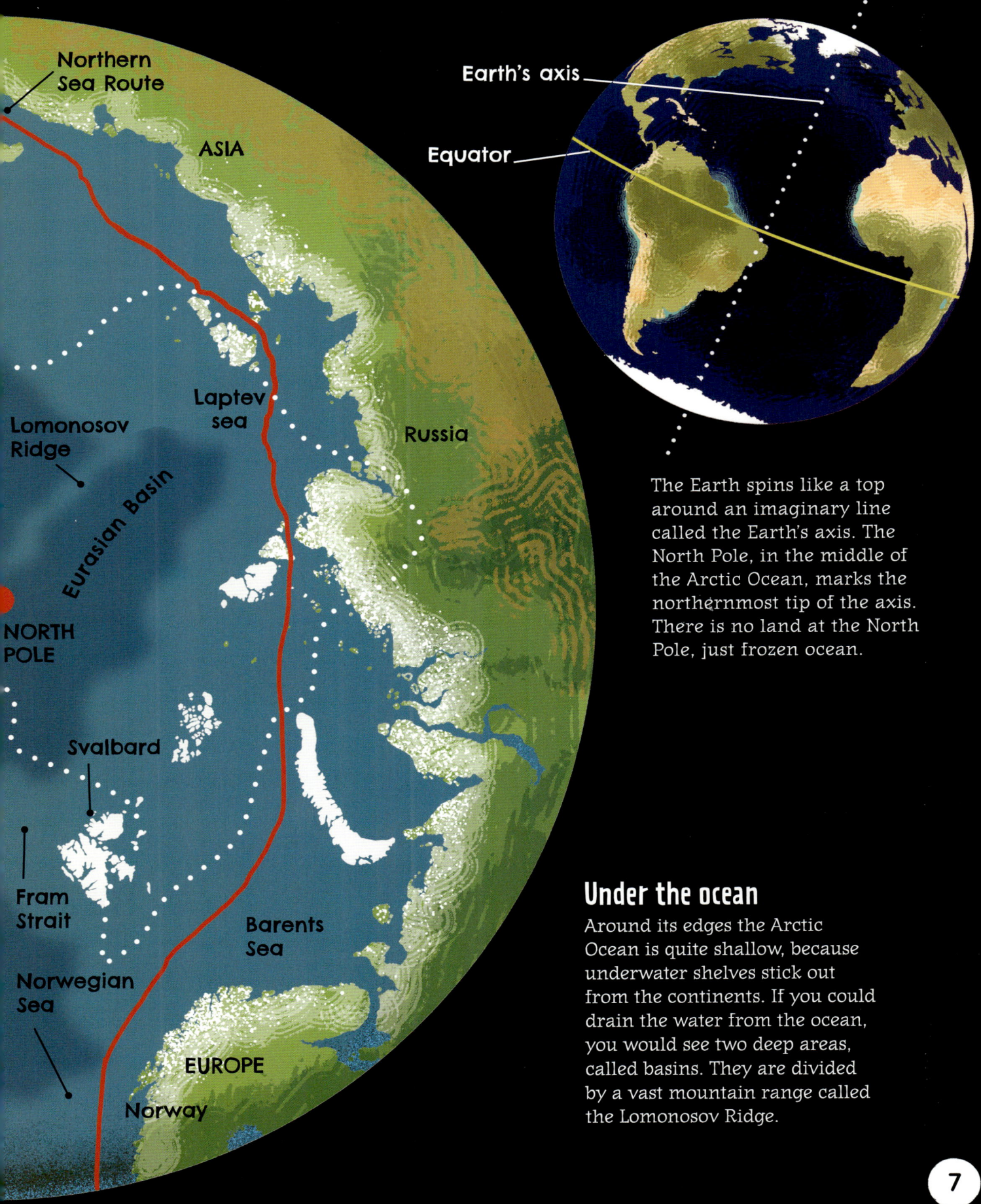

The Earth spins like a top around an imaginary line called the Earth's axis. The North Pole, in the middle of the Arctic Ocean, marks the northernmost tip of the axis. There is no land at the North Pole, just frozen ocean.

Under the ocean

Around its edges the Arctic Ocean is quite shallow, because underwater shelves stick out from the continents. If you could drain the water from the ocean, you would see two deep areas, called basins. They are divided by a vast mountain range called the Lomonosov Ridge.

Chapter 1: Around the oceans

The Atlantic Ocean

The Atlantic lies between the continents of North America and South America to the west, and Europe and Africa to the east. Its northern and southern parts connect to icy, polar oceans.

Atlantic rivers

Many of world's great rivers drain their waters into the Atlantic Ocean. They include the Mississippi, the Amazon, the Congo and the Rhine. Sediment from the Amazon river forms a giant fan on the seabed of the Atlantic.

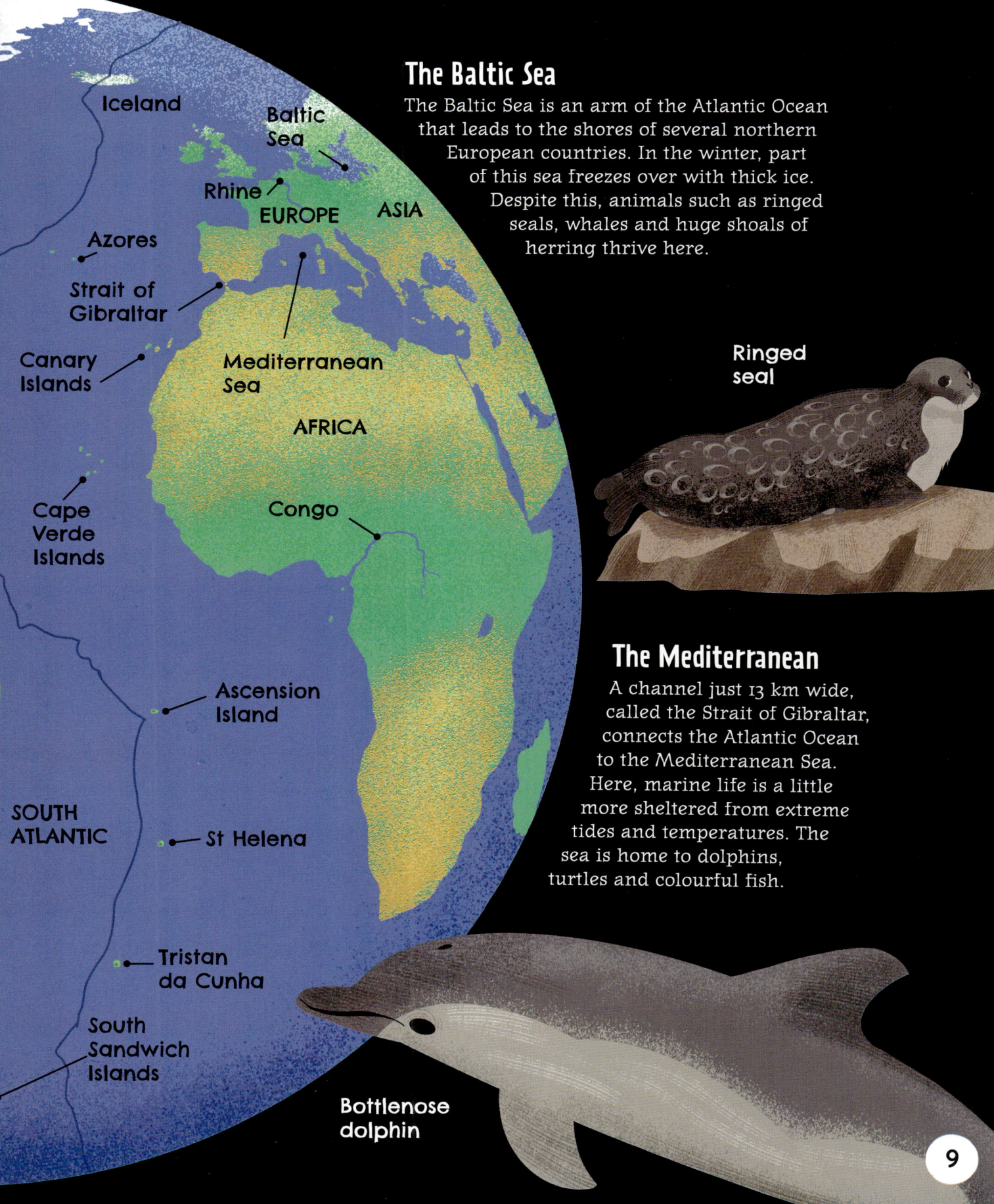

The Baltic Sea

The Baltic Sea is an arm of the Atlantic Ocean that leads to the shores of several northern European countries. In the winter, part of this sea freezes over with thick ice. Despite this, animals such as ringed seals, whales and huge shoals of herring thrive here.

Ringed seal

The Mediterranean

A channel just 13 km wide, called the Strait of Gibraltar, connects the Atlantic Ocean to the Mediterranean Sea. Here, marine life is a little more sheltered from extreme tides and temperatures. The sea is home to dolphins, turtles and colourful fish.

Bottlenose dolphin

The Indian Ocean

The Indian Ocean stretches for more than 10,000 km between the southern tip of Africa and the western coast of Australia. Beneath its waters lie rocky ridges, mountains, valleys and deep trenches.

Ocean ridges

A series of ridges forms a giant upside-down 'Y' on the floor of the Indian Ocean. The seafloor is very slowly spreading along these ridges, as tectonic plates move away from each other. The central ridge is called the Mid-Indian Ocean Ridge.

Seamounts

Steep-sided underwater mountains, known as seamounts, are scattered across the Indian Ocean seafloor. A large group of seamounts lies north of the island of Madagascar. Most seamounts are extinct volcanoes, and can rise to more than 1,000 m above the seafloor.

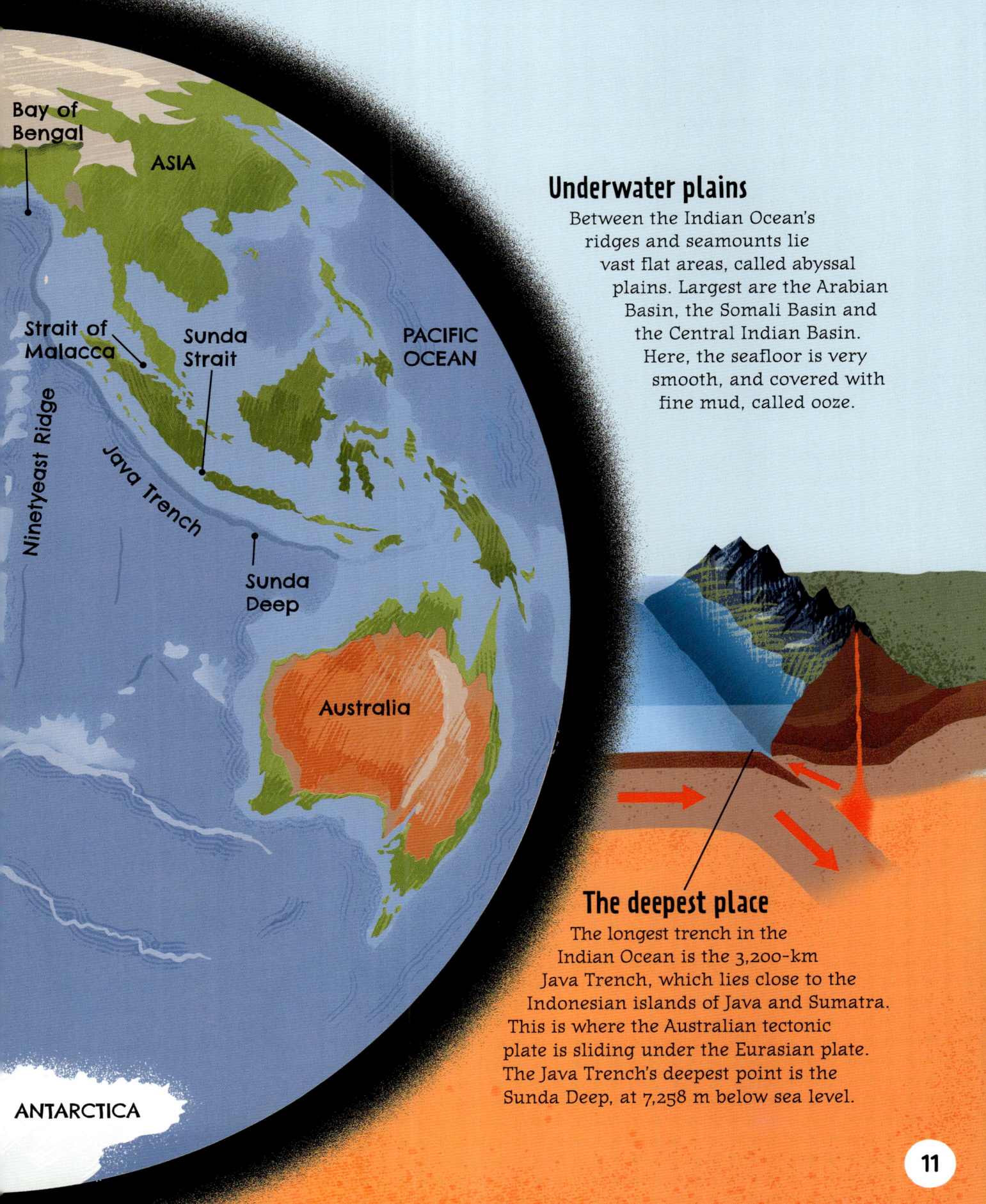

Underwater plains

Between the Indian Ocean's ridges and seamounts lie vast flat areas, called abyssal plains. Largest are the Arabian Basin, the Somali Basin and the Central Indian Basin. Here, the seafloor is very smooth, and covered with fine mud, called ooze.

The deepest place

The longest trench in the Indian Ocean is the 3,200-km Java Trench, which lies close to the Indonesian islands of Java and Sumatra. This is where the Australian tectonic plate is sliding under the Eurasian plate. The Java Trench's deepest point is the Sunda Deep, at 7,258 m below sea level.

The Pacific Ocean

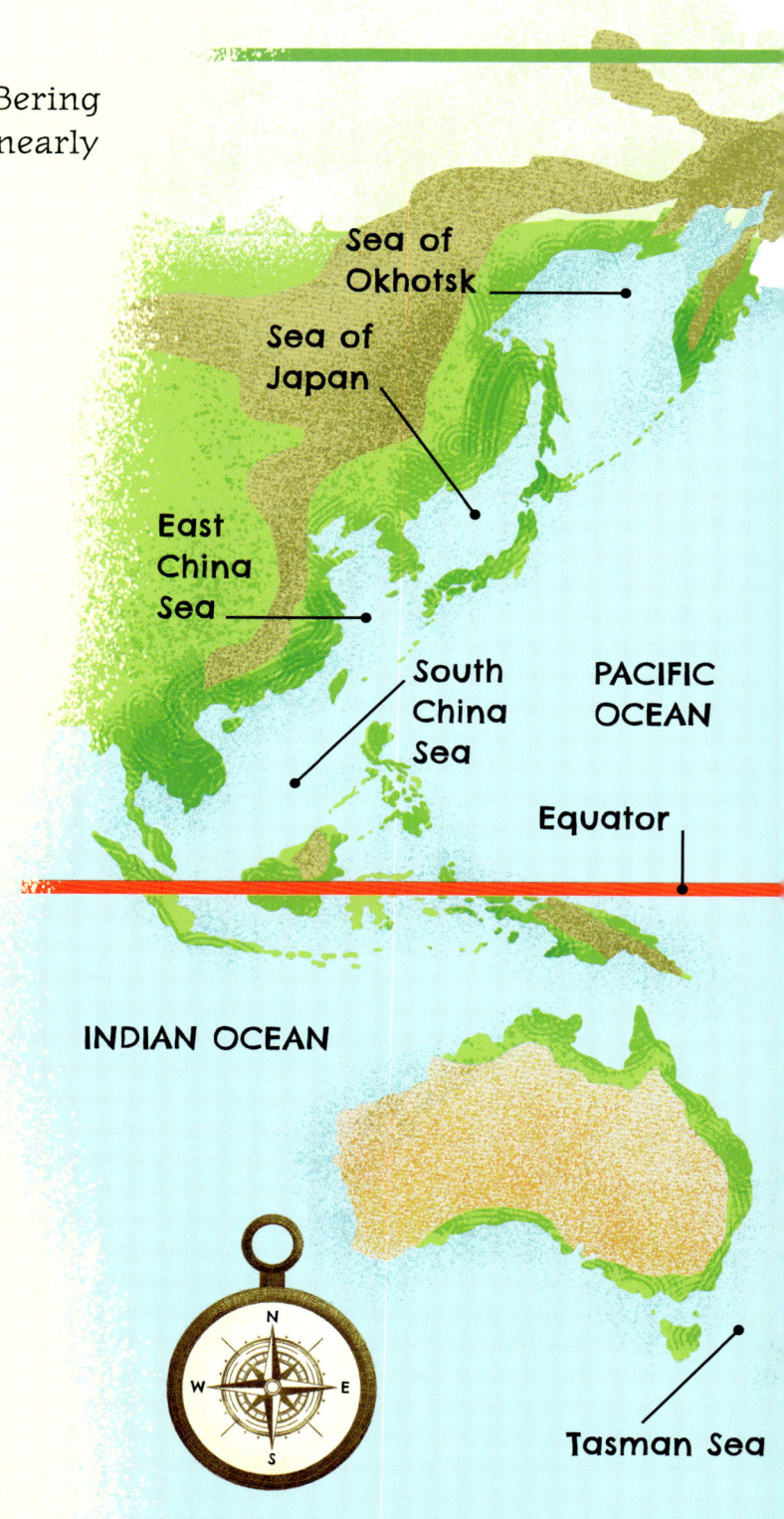

The Pacific stretches from the Southern Ocean in the south to the Bering Strait in the north. Its waters cover nearly one-third of the Earth's surface.

Ocean and seas

The equator divides the Pacific into the North Pacific and South Pacific. Parts of its western section are seas – areas of water surrounded by islands or peninsulas. On the eastern side is the Gulf of California.

Southern edge

The South Pacific ends along the 60° south line of latitude – two-thirds of the way between the equator and the South Pole. All the water that lies to the south of this line is considered to be part of the Southern Ocean.

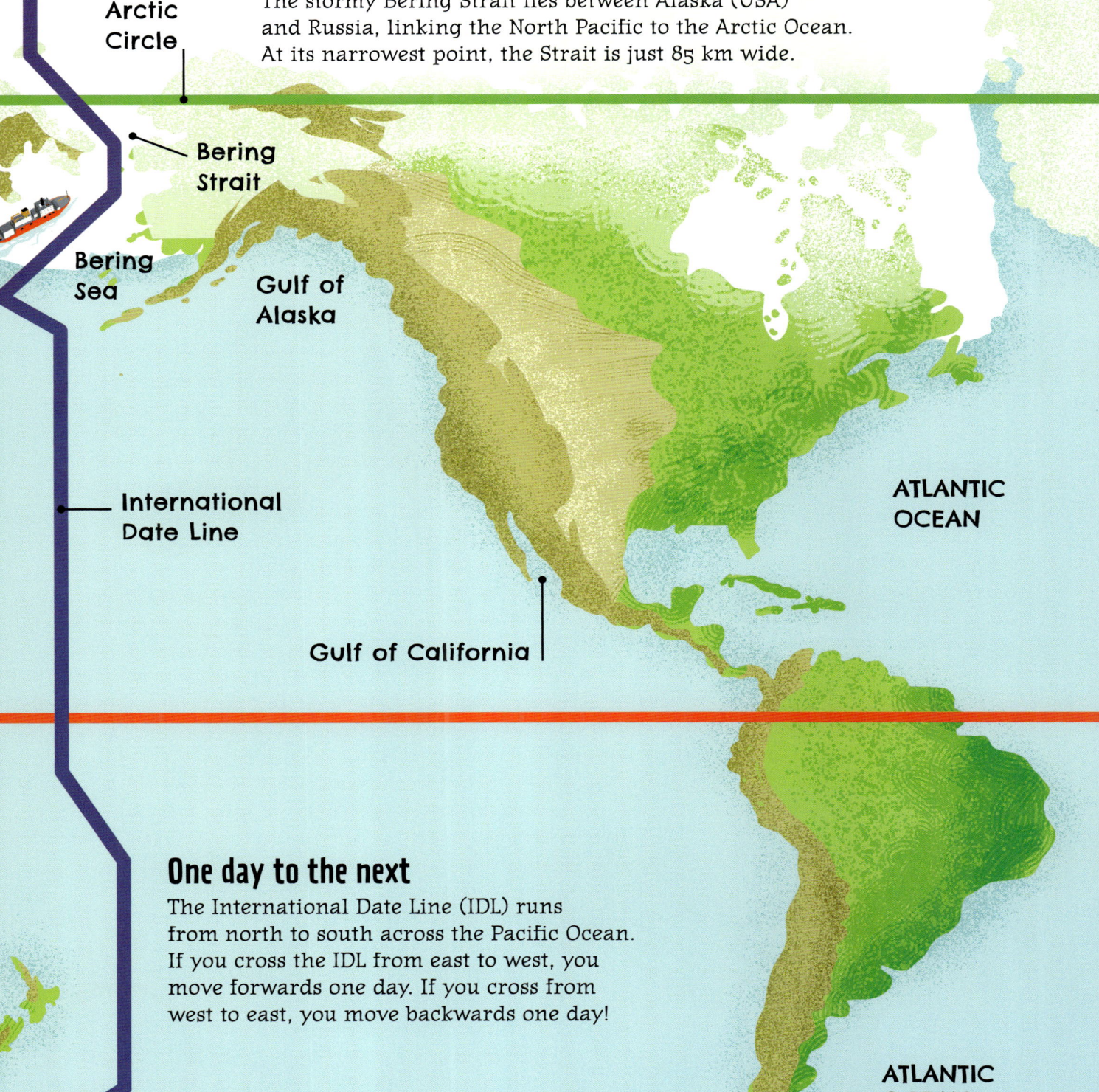

The Southern Ocean

The Southern Ocean sits at the bottom of the world, surrounding the continent of Antarctica. It links the Pacific, Atlantic and Indian Oceans to each other.

The Drake Passage

The Drake Passage is the narrowest part of the Southern Ocean. It was named after the English 16th-century naval explorer Sir Francis Drake. Here, the gap between the southern tip of South America and the South Shetland Islands is just 800 km wide. Strong currents in the Drake Passage whip up stormy seas and giant waves.

The deepest point

The South Sandwich Trench is a deep canyon that stretches 965 km across the floor of the Southern Ocean. Its deepest point lies 7,434 m below the surface. It was explored by a submersible, called *Limiting Factor*, during the Five Deeps Expedition in 2019.

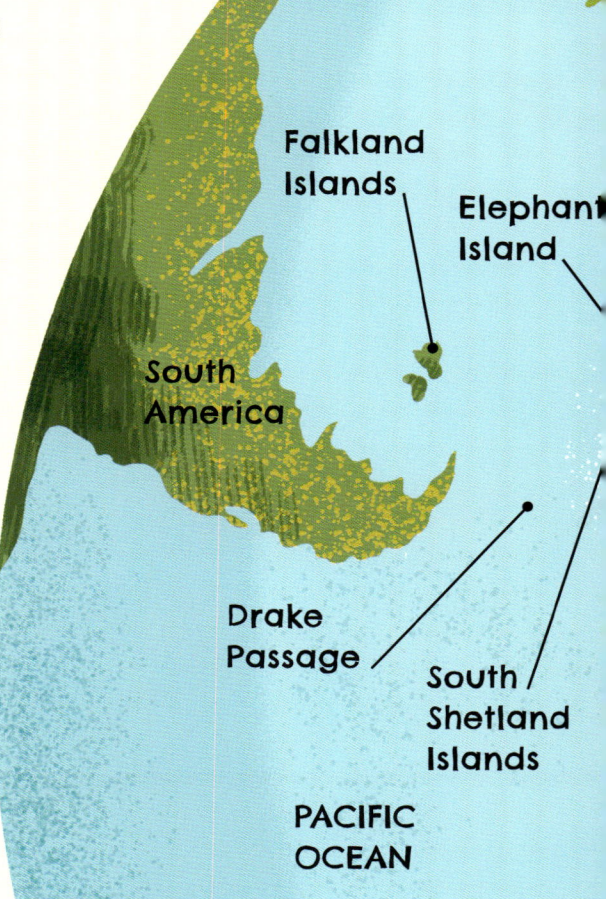

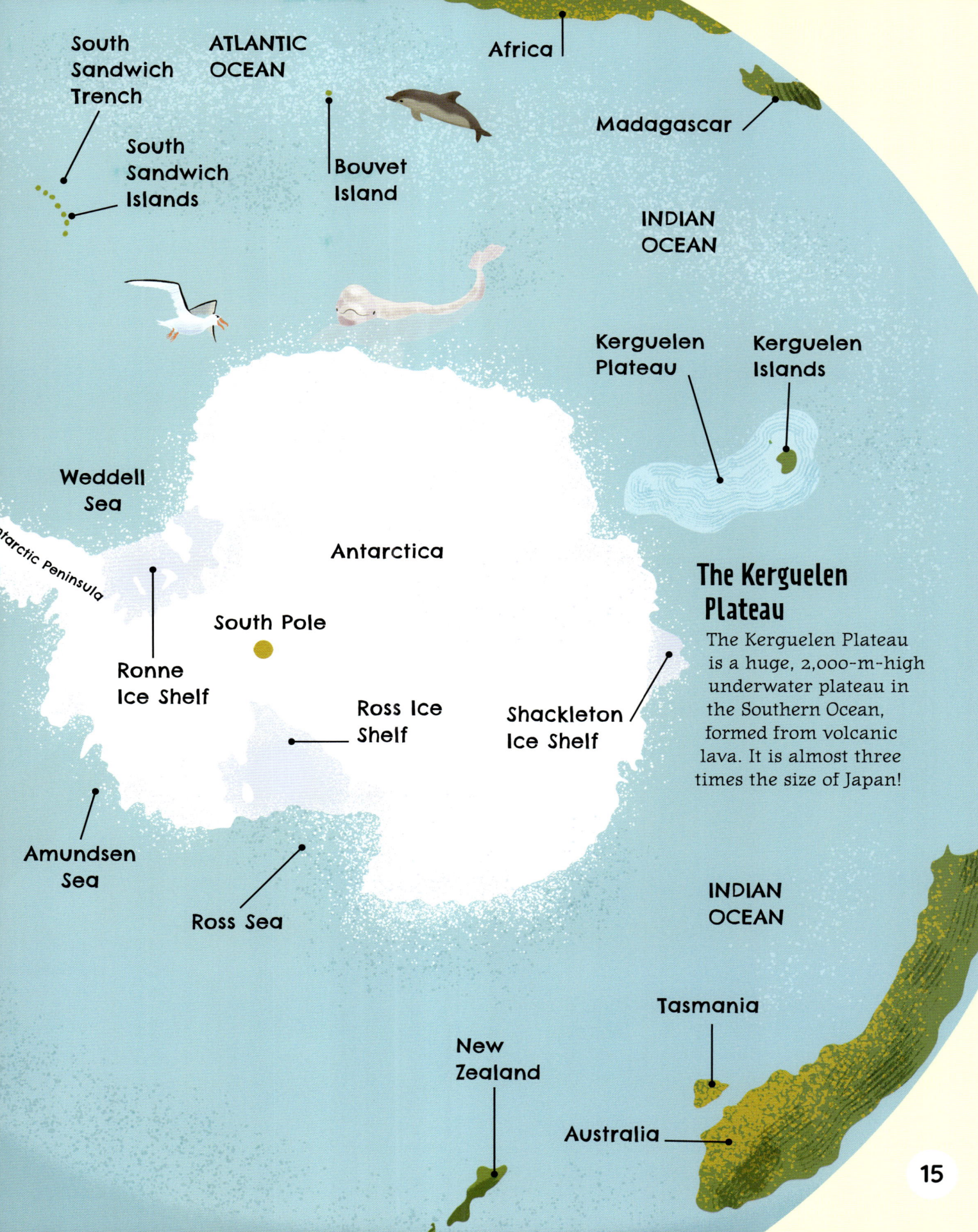

Chapter 2: Unique features

Wind, weather and currents

The waters of the Atlantic are always on the move. Currents carry warm or cold water around the ocean, driven by the wind. These currents affect the climate of the land they flow past and can cause extreme weather events.

Hurricanes

Destructive tropical storms called hurricanes form high above the Atlantic. They begin life as groups of powerful thunderstorms that then start spinning, gathering energy from the warm, tropical waters. When hurricanes meet land, they can destroy whole cities and cause huge floods.

Trades and westerlies

Atlantic wind patterns called trades and westerlies can influence the path of a hurricane. Trade winds form north and south of the equator; further north and south, westerlies blow in the opposite direction. As they form and gather speed, hurricanes often follow the paths of the trades and westerlies.

Atlantic gyres

Currents also often play a part in the formation of a hurricane. Gyres are circular currents north and south of the equator that are driven by winds. Thunderstorms often form above these currents and the winds that accompany them can sometimes develop into hurricanes.

The Gulf Stream

Flowing north from the Gulf of Mexico, the Gulf Stream carries warm water up the eastern coastline of North America, then across to Europe. This brings mild temperatures to the coasts of northern Europe. The warm water of the stream also helps hurricanes form and intensify along its path.

Chapter 2: Unique features

Volcanoes and islands

Along the Mid-Atlantic Ridge, magma rises from beneath the seabed to the surface to form volcanoes. Most of these volcanoes erupt deep under the waves, but some grow high enough to break the surface and form islands.

Iceland

The island of Iceland sits at the northern end of the Mid-Atlantic Ridge. The ridge runs right through the middle of the island, marked by a rocky gorge. As a result, Iceland has many active volcanoes, some hidden under ice caps.

Azores

The Azores lie where the Mid-Atlantic Ridge meets the boundary between the Eurasian plate and African plate. Each of the nine islands is the tip of a giant underwater volcano. Other remote, volcanic Atlantic islands include Ascension Island, St Helena and Tristan da Cunha.

Island arcs

Volcanoes often form close to undersea subduction zones. Magma rises on one side of the zone, creating a line of volcanic islands called an island arc. The South Sandwich Islands in the southern Atlantic and the Lesser Antilles in the Caribbean Sea are island arcs.

Chapter 2: Unique features

The Great Barrier Reef

The shallow, warm waters of the southern Pacific Ocean are home to one of the most incredible habitats on our planet. The Great Barrier Reef is said to be the largest living feature built by animals on Earth.

Growing reefs

The coral polyps that build the Great Barrier Reef are tiny organisms that feed on plankton. As they grow, they deposit limestone around themselves to form a hard case. Together, these cases form rocky reefs.

A living chain

The Great Barrier Reef is made up of thousands of coral reefs and islands stretching for over 2,000 km along Australia's northeast coast. It has taken millions of years for the Great Barrier Reef to form.

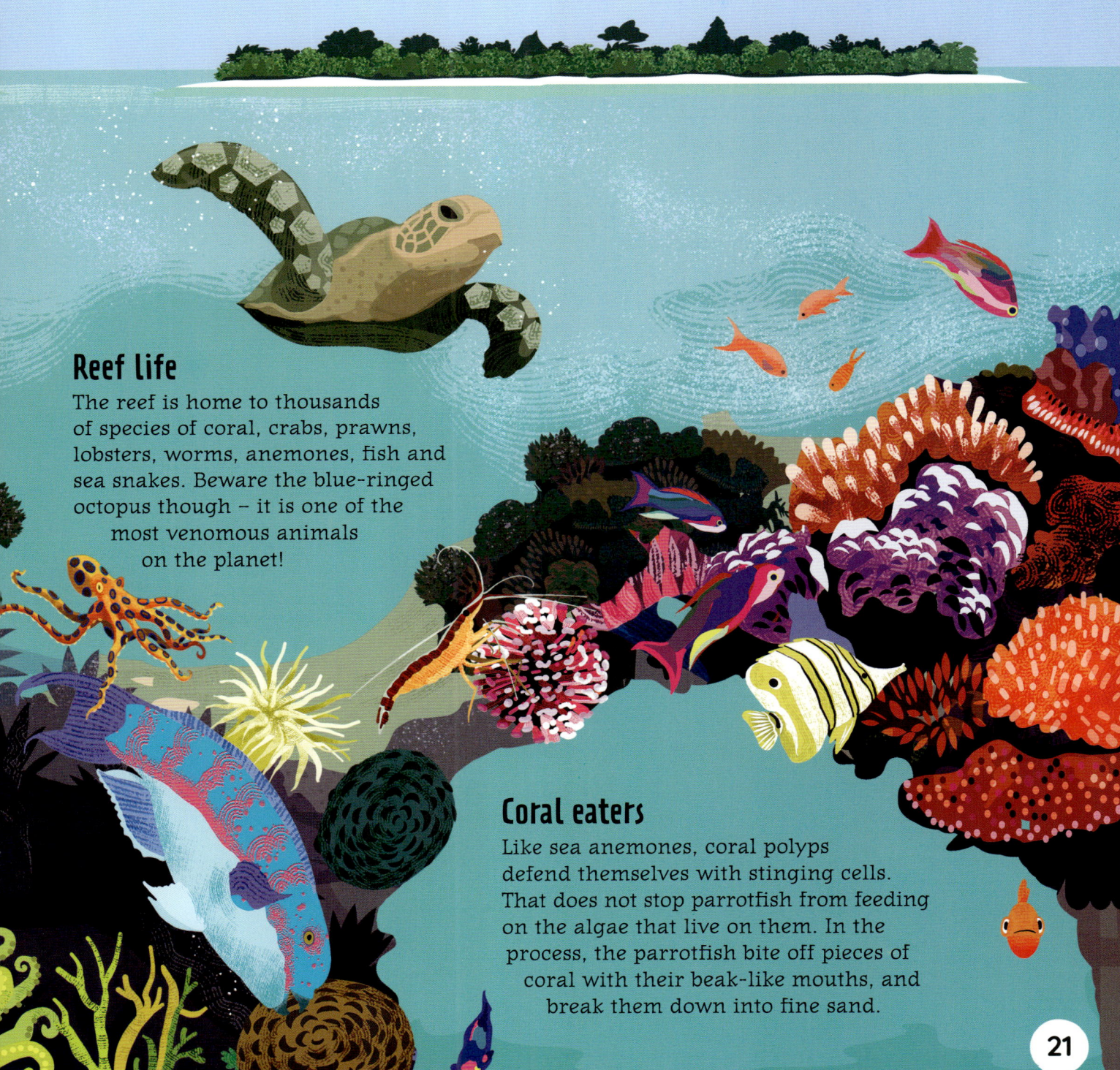

Reef life

The reef is home to thousands of species of coral, crabs, prawns, lobsters, worms, anemones, fish and sea snakes. Beware the blue-ringed octopus though – it is one of the most venomous animals on the planet!

Coral eaters

Like sea anemones, coral polyps defend themselves with stinging cells. That does not stop parrotfish from feeding on the algae that live on them. In the process, the parrotfish bite off pieces of coral with their beak-like mouths, and break them down into fine sand.

Pacific islands

More than 25,000 islands are dotted around the Pacific Ocean. Some are large, and home to millions of people. Others are tiny and uninhabited. Most Pacific islands are either active or extinct volcanoes.

Island groups

There are three main groups of Pacific islands: Melanesia, Micronesia and Polynesia. Melanesia includes the largest Pacific island, New Guinea. The islands of Polynesia form a giant triangle. They include New Zealand and Hawaii.

Island arcs

Many Pacific islands, such as the Aleutians in the north and the Mariana Islands in the west, were fomed by volcanic activity millions of years ago. They are grouped in long, curving island arcs.

The Hawaiian Islands

A chain of around 130 islands stretches from the island of Hawaii itself to Midway Island, more than 2,400 km away. This chain formed as the Pacific plate moved over a 'hot spot' in the Earth's crust. Hawaii itself is the top of an active volcano. The plate is still moving, and so more volcanoes may be formed.

Pacific atolls

Atolls are formed when coral reefs grow around volcanic islands. As the extinct volcano disappears beneath the waves, the reefs are left behind.

Chapter 2: Unique features

An icy ocean

The most southerly parts of the Southern Ocean sit inside the Antarctic Circle. In the middle of winter, the Sun never rises and temperatures can fall below -60°C. Half of the Southern Ocean freezes over entirely with thick sea ice.

Ice fluctuation

In winter, the sea ice stretches more than 1,500 km from the coast of Antarctica. It covers an area of 20,000,000 square km. In spring, as temperatures slowly rise, it melts away again.

Pancakes and pack ice

As the surface of the sea freezes, it often forms icy discs, called pancakes. These grow and overlap to make solid ice, known as pack ice. Pack ice drifts along at up to 20 km a day, carried by ocean currents. It is pushed and shoved by winds and waves. In places, this opens up areas of water, called leads. In others, the ice crunches up into blocks called pressure ridges.

The Ross Ice Shelf

Part of the Ross Sea is covered by a vast sheet of ice, hundreds of metres thick. It is called the Ross Ice Shelf and is about the size of France. The ice moves very slowly out to sea, fed by glaciers flowing down from the Antarctic continent. At the front of the Ross Ice Shelf is a sheer icy cliff, 50 to 60 m high, and 800 km long.

Icebergs

Huge chunks of ice break off from Antarctica's ice shelves and glaciers, forming icebergs. This is known as calving. Winds and currents carry the icebergs out into the Southern Ocean, where they very slowly melt away.

Chapter 2: Unique features

Arctic seasons

The Sun is always low in the sky over the Arctic Ocean. Because of this, the water gets much less heat than if it was closer to the equator, where the Sun climbs higher. This makes the Arctic Ocean one of the coldest places on Earth.

Arctic climate

The Arctic is not only very cold, it is also extremely dry. Only a little snow falls into the Arctic Ocean, and settles on top of the sea ice. The white ice and snow reflect most of the sunlight that reaches the ground, keeping the ice and land cold.

Summer and winter

In the Arctic, there are two main seasons: winter and summer. Winter is very long – it lasts for about nine months, from September to May. In mid-winter, the temperature can fall to lower than −60°C. Summer lasts for just three months (June, July and August), with temperatures by the shore reaching around 0°C, and up to 12°C further inland.

The midnight Sun

The Arctic Circle lies just above the 66° north line of latitude. Inside the Arctic Circle, there are days in mid-winter when the Sun never rises, and days in mid-summer when the Sun never sets. At the North Pole, the Sun only rises and sets once a year, on the equinox.

Chapter 3: Voyages of discovery

Triangular Trade

Crossing the Atlantic

Vikings were the first Europeans to sail across the Atlantic. They landed in Iceland in the 870s and Greenland in the 980s. In around 1000, they reached North America.

New contact

In 1492, Italian navigator Christopher Columbus set out across the Atlantic to discover new trade routes to Asia. Instead, he arrived in the Americas, which were already home to millions of indigenous peoples. This marked the beginning of the colonisation of the Americas by Europeans.

Trade and slavery

From the 1600s, Europeans transported enslaved people from Africa across the Atlantic to work for settlers in the Americas. The crops grown by enslaved Africans were then shipped back to Europe to produce goods such as sugar and cotton cloth. These were sold to buy and enslave more African people. This was known as the Triangular Trade as it followed a roughly triangular route.

Undersea discoveries

The exploration of what lay under the Atlantic began in the 1870s, with an expedition by a British naval ship, HMS *Challenger*. Scientists on the *Challenger* confirmed the existence of the Mid-Atlantic Ridge. Further mapping of the ridge in the 1950s helped scientists to prove the theory of plate tectonics.

Chapter 3: Voyages of discovery

Exploring the Pacific

The Pacific has a long history of exploration. It began thousands of years ago, when sea-faring people from southeast Asia sailed out in search of new lands to settle.

The Polynesians

Around 4,000 years ago, explorers from southeast Asia set sail in outrigger canoes. They navigated by observing the stars, waves and clouds. Within 3,000 years, these peoples, now known as Polynesians, had discovered and settled nearly all of the Pacific islands.

Cook's voyages

In the 1760s and 1770s, British navigator James Cook made three voyages around the Pacific Ocean. Cook was the first person to make accurate maps of the area. He also began the era of European colonisation of many South Pacific countries.

Darwin and the *Beagle*

Charles Darwin was a naturalist on board the HMS *Beagle* when it sailed around the world in the 1830s. During a stop at the Galápagos Islands, off the coast of South America, Darwin studied the unique plants and animals. This helped him to develop his ground-breaking theory of evolution.

Into the depths

In the 1870s, the crew of British naval ship HMS *Challenger* made the first scientific study of the Pacific Ocean depths. By dredging the ocean floor as far as 8,000 m down, they discovered thousands of new species of animal. This marked the beginning of the science of oceanography.

Chapter 3: Voyages of discovery

Arctic journeys

The indigenous peoples of the Arctic were the first people to explore the Arctic Ocean. In the last few hundred years, explorers from other parts of the world have ventured across the ice and reached the North Pole. Many only stayed alive because they learned survival skills from the local people.

Viking voyages

Just over a thousand years ago, Viking explorers sailed along the edges of the Arctic Ocean. They discovered Iceland and Greenland, and established settlements there. They also sailed north around Scandinavia, and may have reached Svalbard, deep into the Arctic Ocean.

Through the ice
From the 16th century onwards, English and Dutch traders searched for shortcuts through the Arctic Ocean to connect the Atlantic and Pacific Oceans. None of the searches were successful. Norwegian explorer Roald Amundsen finally found a route through in 1903.

Race to the pole
Explorers from Europe and North America were keen to be the first to reach the North Pole. In 1896, Norwegian explorer Fridtjof Nansen came within 370 km of the pole. The first people on record to reach the pole were probably Americans Robert Peary and Matthew Henson, along with four Inuit guides, in 1909.

Modern exploration
Scientists have set up stations on research ships in the Arctic Ocean to study the ice, wildlife, climate and the changes that global warming is causing to the area. Scientists even scuba dive through holes in the ice to study what is happening below the waves.

Indian Ocean explorers

Exploration of the Indian Ocean most likely began tens of thousands of years ago, when people settled on the coasts and islands of the Indian Ocean. This exploration continued in ancient times, as traders sailed between towns and cities along the Indian Ocean coast.

Arab dhows

As early as the 1st century CE, sailors and merchants from the Middle East were planning their trading voyages to take advantage of the monsoon winds and currents. The sailors knew the best times of the year to sail their dhows from India to Arabia and Africa in order to avoid storms. They had detailed knowledge of the Indian Ocean's ports and the best goods to trade.

Zheng He

Between 1405 and 1433, Chinese explorer Zheng He made seven voyages from China into the Indian Ocean, commanding huge fleets of ships that carried thousands of men. He explored the lands of the Persian Gulf and the coast of Africa, returning home with treasures and wild animals.

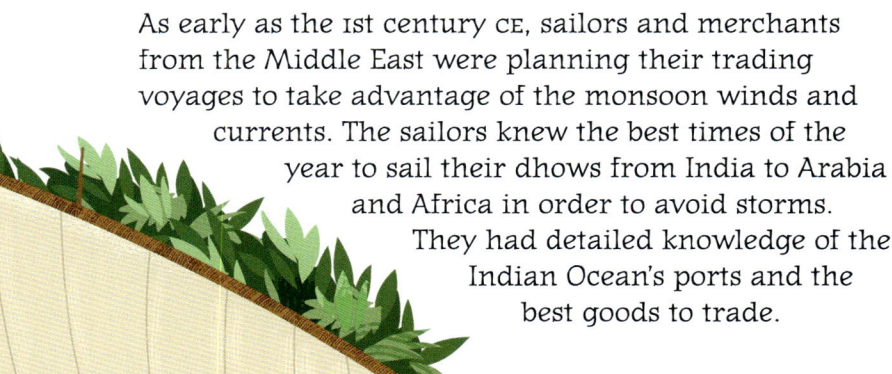

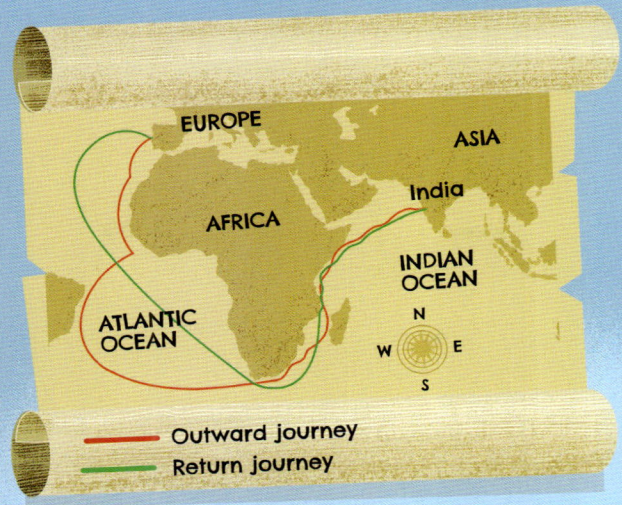

Vasco da Gama

In 1497, Portuguese navigator Vasco da Gama became the first European explorer to sail from the Atlantic Ocean to the Indian Ocean. Over the following centuries, the Dutch, French and English established trading posts and colonised many areas around the Indian Ocean.

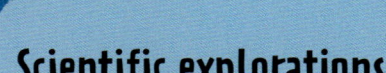

Scientific explorations

In the 1960s, the International Indian Ocean Expedition became the first to explore the climate, currents, wildlife and underwater volcanoes of the Indian Ocean. Modern expeditions use submersibles and autonomous underwater gilders, such as *Challenger*, to dive down to the depths of the Indian Ocean.

Chapter 3: Voyages of discovery

Southern science

Nobody lives in Antarctica permanently, but research ships carry scientists from around the world into the Southern Ocean to study its deep, cold waters and the wildlife that lives in them. Many also live in research stations on the Antarctic continent.

Research stations

Several countries have research stations in Antarctica. The UK's remote Halley VI Research Station sits on the floating ice of the Brunt Ice Shelf on the Weddell Sea. Its laboratories and accommodation are housed in eight pods. These sit on skis, so they can be slid to safety if the ice underneath them cracks!

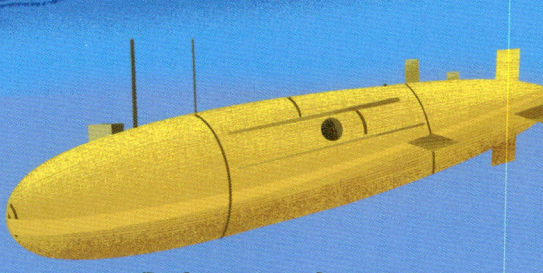

Robots and remotes

Some research ships carry underwater machines called Remotely Operated Vehicles (ROVs). These craft dive down to explore the seabed under the ice and take a visual record of it.

Research ships

Specially built ice-breaking ships take scientists out into the Southern Ocean. On board, there are science laboratories, instruments, such as weather stations, and echo sounders for mapping the seafloor and searching for marine animals. Nets and drills are used for collecting samples from the water and the seabed.

Visiting the ocean floor

Autonomous Underwater Vehicles (AUVs) and manned submersibles dive hundreds or thousands of metres down to visit the ocean floor. They have discovered that along the Antarctic coast, the seabed is busy with life, such as feather stars, sea cucumbers and icefish.

Life in the Arctic

Animals found in and around the Arctic Ocean have adapted to life in the extreme cold. Many mammals have layers of fat (blubber), or thick fur, to keep them warm.

Walruses

Walruses collect in herds on the sea ice and nearby coasts. They dive down to forage for clams, snails, worms and crabs on the sea floor. Males use their long tusks for fighting, self-defence and to keep breathing holes open in the ice.

Beluga whales

Belugas are small whales that can grow up to 6 m long. They are easy to recognise thanks to their distinctive white colouring. As they swim, belugas send out sounds through their bulbous heads, and listen for echoes. This helps them to find gaps in the sea ice where they can breathe..

Ringed seals

The ringed seal is one of the most common Arctic seals. Others include the harp and ribbon seal. Like all these seals, ringed seals are born and live on ice floes. They dip under the ice to hide from the polar bears that hunt them.

Narwhals

Narwhals live in the Arctic Ocean all year round, close to the pack ice. All male narwhals and a few females have a long, spiraled tusk, which is actually an overgrown tooth. Scientists think that the tusk may be for attracting a mate or scaring off rival narwhals, but they do not know for certain.

Pacific animals

An extraordinary range of animals live in and around the Pacific Ocean. Some live there all year round. Others just pass through on their annual migrations.

Grey whales

In the Northern Hemisphere's summer, grey whales search for food in the Bering Sea. In autumn, they travel south to the Gulf of California to breed and rear their young. The following spring, they head back north, and complete their 20,000-km round trip.

Pacific salmon

The life of a Pacific salmon begins in a freshwater river or lake in North America. After growing into a small fish called a smolt, it swims to the sea, where it adapts to living in saltwater. After two or more years of growing into an adult fish, it returns to the place of its birth to breed.

Leatherback turtles

The world's largest species of turtle, the leatherback, can weigh up to a tonne. Brilliant long-distance swimmers, leatherbacks travel thousands of kilometres in their lifetime between their feeding and breeding grounds. They are also excellent divers, reaching depths of 1,200 m to hunt for jellyfish, their favourite food.

Glow-in-the-dark

Below about 1,000 m, the waters of the Pacific are pitch black and a lot colder than at the surface. The creatures that live here have adapted to the darkness and are often bioluminescent – they create their own light to lure prey.

Chapter 4: Ocean wildlife

Pacific plants

While animals live throughout the Pacific Ocean, plants can only grow in places where they can get enough light to make their food, such as in shallow waters, on reefs, near the surface or along rocky coastlines.

Phytoplankton

Microscopic plants, called phytoplankton, live in the upper few hundred metres of the ocean. They are at the bottom of most Pacific food chains, and are eaten by small fish and other animals. As phytoplankton make food for themselves, they take in carbon dioxide and give out oxygen.

Kelp forests

Kelp is a type of seaweed that grows well in the shallow, cold waters of the eastern Pacific coast. Along the coasts of California and Canada, giant kelp grows in strands up to 65 m long, creating thick, underwater forests.

Life among the kelp

Sea otters hunt for shellfish and sea urchins among the kelp, breaking them open on stones balanced on their chests. Small fish and invertebrates shelter among the strands of kelp. They are hunted by larger animals, such as seals and sea lions.

Eelgrass

Seagrasses grow along coasts, forming large mats on the seabed. Eelgrass is a type of seagrass that grows along the Pacific coast of North America. It is an important habitat for the young of some fish, such as herring.

Penguin power

The Southern Ocean's most famous inhabitants are its penguins. Many different species of these unique black and white birds live in and around Antarctica.

Adaptations for the cold

Penguins are well adapted to the cold weather and icy seas around Antarctica. Their overlapping feathers form a waterproof outer layer. Below this are two insulating layers – one of fluffy feathers, and one of fat – found under the skin.

Underwater fliers

Penguins cannot fly. Instead, they swim or 'fly' through the water, hunting fish, squid and krill. They use their wings as flippers. On land, penguins waddle, or slide along on their bellies.

Adelie penguin

King penguin

Emperor penguin

Caring fathers

The biggest of the penguins, emperor penguins breed on the sea ice in the middle of winter. Females lay their eggs, then head off to the sea to feed. Males keep the precious eggs warm for two months, balanced on their feet and tucked under a flap of skin, called a brood pouch. They all huddle tightly together for warmth.

Macaroni penguin

Breeding colonies

Penguins live on rocky or grassy shores, on beaches and on sea ice. They gather in breeding colonies, called rookeries. One rookery may contain tens of thousands of birds. Here, the penguins are safe from leopard seals and orcas. But these predators lie in wait when the penguins go hunting in the ocean.

Indian Ocean animals

An enormous range of animals lives in the Indian Ocean. At the bottom of every ocean food chain are microscopic phytoplankton, and tiny animals, called zooplankton.

Lively reefs

There are lots of coral reefs along the shores of the Indian Ocean, and many islands are themselves formed from coral. Coral reefs are the habitat of a vast range of marine animals, such as crabs, sea urchins, starfish and colourful reef fish.

Reef manta rays

The world's largest group of reef manta rays lives in the waters around the Maldives. In summer and autumn, hundreds of these rays gather to eat the blooms of zooplankton.

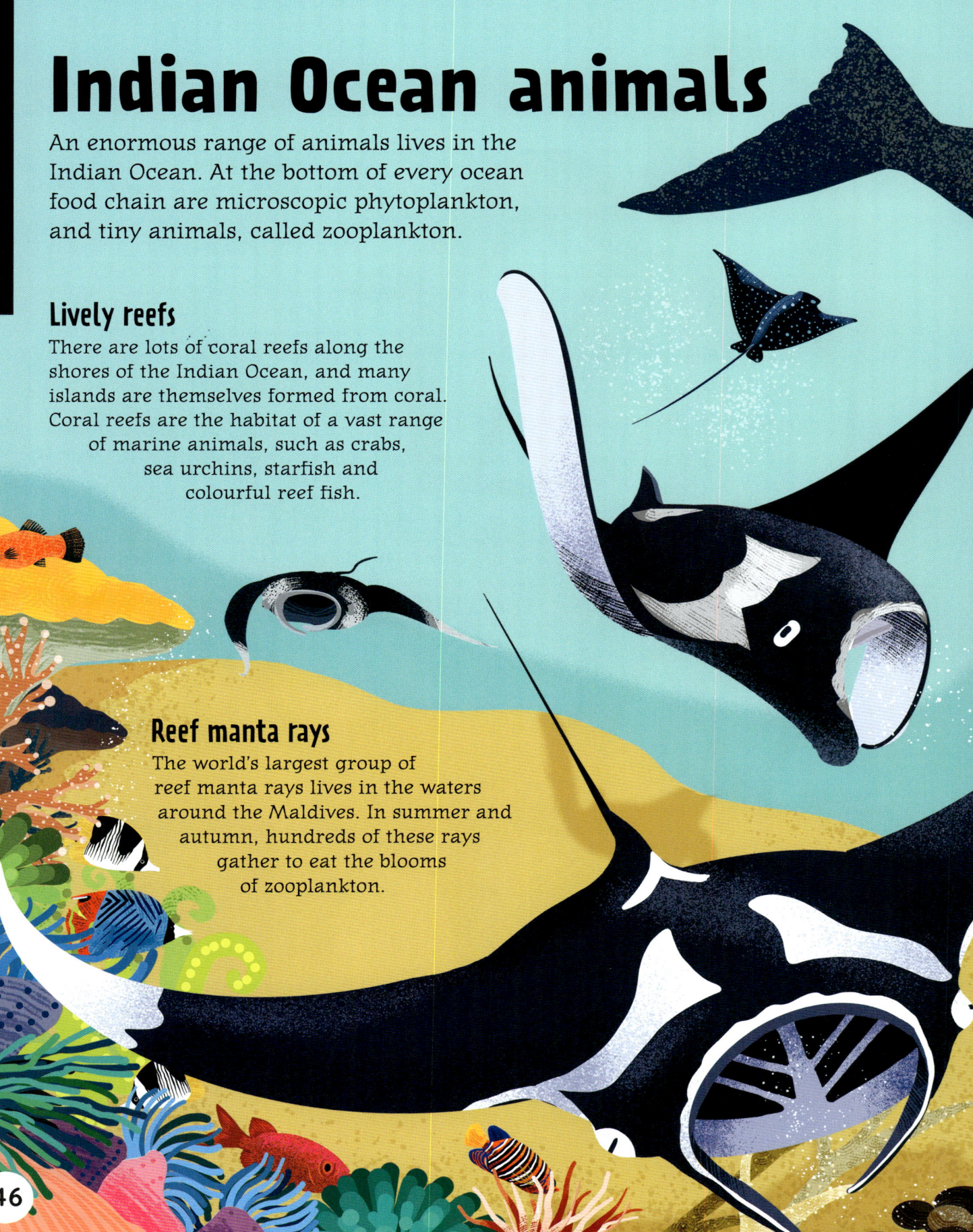

Dugong

The dugong is a slow-moving mammal that grazes on sea grasses in the shallow coastal waters of the Indian Ocean. Also known as sea cows, and closely related to elephants, dugongs can grow up to 3 m long. In the past, sailors sometimes mistook them for mermaids!

Ancient survivor

The coelacanth is a big, bony type of fish that was thought to have become extinct millions of years ago. Then, in 1938, one was caught in the southern Indian Ocean, and many others have since been found.

Chapter 4: Ocean wildlife

Atlantic green turtles

Some animals travel long distances through Atlantic waters in their lifetime, searching for food, or migrating to their breeding grounds. Among them are Atlantic green turtles.

Feeding and breeding

Green turtles spend most of their lives grazing on coastal seagrass. Every few years, they return to the beaches where they hatched, so that they can breed. Some of these migrations are over 2,000 km long.

Laying eggs

At the beach, a female turtle digs a hole in the sand, above the high-tide line. Then she lays hundreds of eggs in her nest. After laying her eggs, she returns to the sea, and swims away.

Hatchlings

The eggs hatch around six to eight weeks later. The hatchlings usually emerge at night to avoid the heat of the Sun. As they make their way to the sea, many are eaten by gulls and crabs. Those who survive will one day travel back here to breed themselves.

Chapter 5: Looking ahead

Indian Ocean riches

The Indian Ocean is packed with valuable resources. These include fish and other marine animals, minerals, crops grown on the coasts and islands, and the beauty of the ocean itself.

Fisheries

In the shallow coastal waters of the Indian Ocean, local people catch shrimps and fish using traditional fishing methods. In Sri Lanka, fishermen perch on stilt-like poles, dangling their fishing rods into the sea. In deeper, offshore waters, large fishing boats catch huge netfuls of shrimp, tuna and billfish.

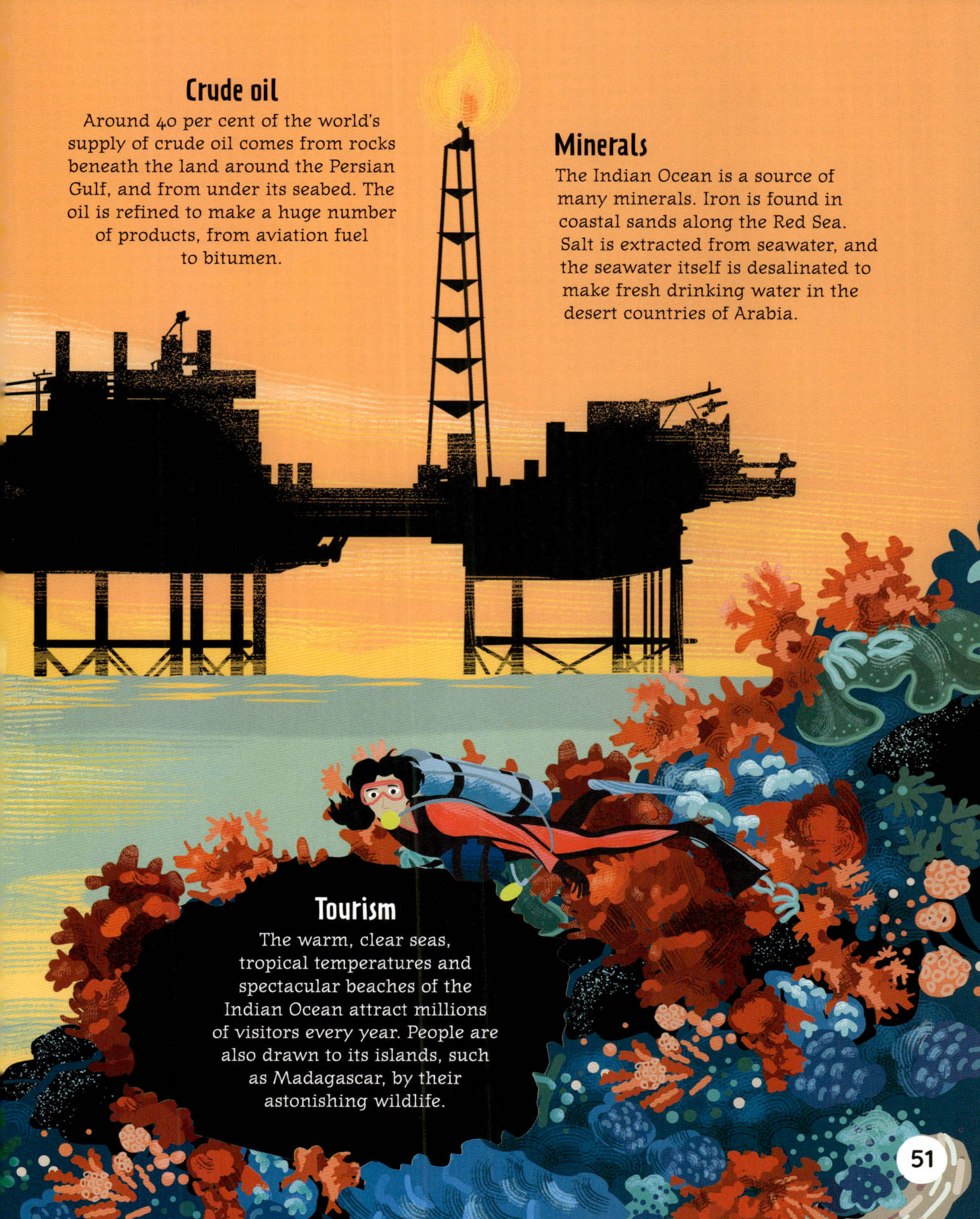

Crude oil

Around 40 per cent of the world's supply of crude oil comes from rocks beneath the land around the Persian Gulf, and from under its seabed. The oil is refined to make a huge number of products, from aviation fuel to bitumen.

Minerals

The Indian Ocean is a source of many minerals. Iron is found in coastal sands along the Red Sea. Salt is extracted from seawater, and the seawater itself is desalinated to make fresh drinking water in the desert countries of Arabia.

Tourism

The warm, clear seas, tropical temperatures and spectacular beaches of the Indian Ocean attract millions of visitors every year. People are also drawn to its islands, such as Madagascar, by their astonishing wildlife.

Chapter 5: Looking ahead

Indian Ocean in danger

The Indian Ocean and its people, plants and animals face many environmental problems. Most of these problems have been brought about by human activity.

Ocean pollution

Waste from factories and homes is washed down rivers, blown or dumped into the Indian Ocean. Plastic waste washes up on beaches, or is carried around by winds and currents. Because of the large number of tankers, oil spills are always a risk. Spilt oil harms ocean wildlife. It also pollutes areas where humans live and source their food.

Wildlife threats

Overfishing and accidental catches of animals (called bycatch) mean that animals including dugongs, and some species of shark, dolphin, whale and turtle are in danger of becoming extinct.

Sea-level rise

The world is slowly getting hotter, as humans pump more greenhouse gases into the atmosphere by burning fossil fuels. Global warming is melting glaciers and ice caps, and warm water takes up more space, all of which leads to rising sea levels. This is an urgent problem in the Indian Ocean because it is surrounded by so much low-lying coastland.

The future

Although the Indian Ocean is facing challenges, many people and organisations are working to stop more damage being done. More and more areas are now protected from further development. Places threatened by sea-level rise are adapting. For example, a new flood-proof artificial island, Hulhumale, has been built in the Maldives. These efforts should help to protect the people and wildlife of the Indian Ocean into the future.

Chapter 5: Looking ahead

Atlantic future

It is difficult for scientists to predict exactly what will happen to the Atlantic and its wildlife in the future. There are efforts to stop more harm by protecting animals, reducing pollution and cleaning up the damage already done. But there is a very long way to go.

Increasing temperatures

We are already seeing the effects of global warming in the Atlantic, where the sea temperature has increased by 0.58°C since the 1950s. Even such a small change has a huge effect on wildlife. For example, the number of lobsters living along the coast of North America has dropped, as the lobsters have moved to deeper, colder water.

Rising seas

Global warming is also causing glaciers and ice caps to melt, pouring more water into the oceans. The Atlantic sea level has already risen by about 15 cm since 1995. Without action to stop global warming, those levels might reach 2 m by the end of this century, which would be devastating for low-lying coastlines and their communities.

Cleaning up

In many countries, efforts are being made to reduce the amount of waste going into the Atlantic. Organisations such as Ocean Cleanup and Ocean Conservancy also plan to clean up the plastic rubbish already there.

Reversing the decline

Following the introduction of new fishing rules, some species are recovering after years of decline. Numbers of grey seals, and the white sharks that feed on them, declined in the 1980s and 1990s, but are now recovering well.

Chapter 5: Looking ahead

The changing Arctic

Today, the Arctic Ocean is changing fast. The ice is retreating quickly, people's traditional lives are being disrupted and animals are under threat. The race to save the Arctic is well and truly on.

A warmer world

There are international efforts to slow down, stop and reverse global warming. Most countries are working to reduce their carbon emissions. But, for some time to come, the effects of global warming are likely to get worse.

Indigenous peoples

The loss of sea ice affects the lives of the Inuit and other indigenous Arctic peoples. Traditional hunting and fishing is more difficult and thinner ice is riskier to cross. The lack of winter ice allows storms to whip up waves that cause erosion along the coast. Both the storms and the resulting erosion are a threat to people's homes.

Open Arctic

The loss of sea ice will open the Arctic Ocean to increased shipping, which could lead to more ports being developed on its coasts. A warmer, ice-free Arctic Ocean would also make it easier to drill for oil and gas, and to mine for minerals. Both risk causing pollution and damage to the Arctic's fragile environment.

The Arctic Council

Set up in 1996, the Arctic Council is an organisation made up of members from the countries around the Arctic Ocean and the region's indigenous peoples. Working together, they monitor and tackle the challenges facing the Arctic and strive to protect this unique and precious place for the future.

Chapter 5: Looking ahead

Saving the Southern Ocean

We are already seeing the damage that human activities are causing to the Southern Ocean and the shores of Antarctica. Can anything be done to prevent more problems in this amazing environment?

More warming

Governments around the world are taking action to slow down global warming. But it is likely that temperatures around Antarctica will carry on rising for now, leading to more melting of ice sheets, glaciers and ice caps, and a reduction in winter sea ice. In turn, this will lead to rising sea levels and flooding across the planet.

Past and future

Finding out how the climate around the Southern Ocean has changed in the past helps scientists to understand how it might change in the future. By analysing cores of Antarctic ice, scientists can tell what the climate was like hundreds or even thousands of years ago. They can use this knowledge to predict the future climate.

Success story

When countries work together, the Southern Ocean and its wildlife can be protected. By the 1970s, humans had hunted the blue whale almost to extinction. In 1986, whaling was banned, and blue whales began to make a comeback. It will take centuries for their numbers to recover, but they have been seen feeding around South Georgia again.

The oceans in facts and figures

- Seawater is salty because it contains dissolved minerals such as sodium chloride. The minerals have been washed into the sea from the land over millions of years.

- The area of the Pacific is 155 million square km – about the same as all the Earth's landmasses put together.

- An iceberg labelled Iceberg B-15 was the largest ever recorded. Measuring 295 km by 37 km, it broke off the Ross Ice Shelf in the year 2000.

- It is estimated that there are around 500 million tonnes of krill in the Southern Ocean.

- The most powerful tropical cyclone ever recorded was Typhoon Tip, which hit the Pacific in 1979. It measured 2,200 km across.

- An emperor penguin has been recorded diving to an incredible 535 m below sea level.

- The Mid-Atlantic Ridge is the longest mountain range in the world, although it is mostly hidden under the sea.

- Around 18,000 ships pass through the Suez Canal each year.

- Less snow falls in the Arctic Ocean than rain in the Sahara Desert.

- Many Pacific islands have unique plants and wildlife because they have been cut off from the mainland for so long. The Galápagos Islands are home to marine iguanas, found nowhere else in the world.

- The bottom of the Challenger Deep is much deeper (at 10,925 m below sea level) than the summit of Everest is high (at 8,848 m above sea level).

- The waters of the North Atlantic are the saltiest of all the oceans. Much of the salt, dissolved in the water, flows out of the Mediterranean Sea.

- The earthquake that caused the 2004 Indian Ocean tsunami had a magnitude of 9.1, making it one of the most powerful ever recorded.

- Half of all the oxygen produced by the world's plants comes from phytoplankton as they make food.

- The world's tectonic plates move extremely slowly. The Atlantic is growing wider, but only at a rate of around 1 to 10 cm per year.

- Each spring, as the Sun gets stronger after winter, there is an explosion in the amount of phytoplankton (plant plankton) in the North Atlantic. This is called the spring bloom.

- The dodo was a large flightless bird that lived only on the Indian Ocean island of Mauritius. It became extinct by 1681 after being hunted by humans who landed on the islands, and by introduced animals such as dogs and cats.

- Modern Polynesian fishermen still use the traditional navigation skills passed down to them by their ancestors.

- Each year, the Arctic tern spends spring and summer in the Arctic, before migrating to the Antarctic, 30,000 km away.

- At Thingvellir in Iceland, a narrow, rocky valley shows where the Mid-Atlantic Ridge crosses the island. For centuries, this was the site of Iceland's parliament, the Althing.

- Most reef-making corals have algae growing in their bodies. The algae provide the corals with minerals and give them their colour.

- South Georgia in the Southern Ocean is governed by the UK and has its own postage stamps, even though nobody lives there!

- In medieval times, some people thought that narwhal tusks were unicorn horns.

- Tristan da Cunha is the Atlantic's most isolated inhabited island. Its closest neighbour is St Helena, some 2,120 km away.

- The North Pole lies 700 km across the ocean from the nearest land.

- Oyster beds in the Red Sea were an important source of natural pearls in the past, starting in ancient Egyptian times. Today almost all pearls are grown in pearl farms.

- The Greenland ice sheet contains 30 million cubic km of ice. If all this ice were to melt, sea levels across the world would rise by 6 m.

- Only about ten per cent of an iceberg can be seen; the rest lies under the water.

- The name Atlantic comes from 'Sea of Atlas' – the ancient Greek name for the waters beyond the Mediterranean Sea.

- Polar bears can swim huge distances using their huge front paws as paddles. A polar bear was once spotted 320 km from land!

- The Pacific might not be around for ever. The Earth's tectonic plates will continue to drift and shift for hundreds of millions of years. One day, in the distant future, the Pacific Ocean may close up, and disappear.

Glossary

atoll ring-shaped island formed from coral

basin bowl-shaped dip in the surface of the Earth

bloom rapid growth of microscopic organisms such as phytoplankton

colonisation taking control of another country and making a settlement there

current flow of water in a particular direction

cyclone tropical storm that rotates around a calm central area; also called a hurricane or typhoon

ecosystem plants, animals and the habitat they live in

erosion gradual wearing away of the Earth's surface, for example by wind or water

evaporate turn from liquid into gas when heated

evolution the gradual changes of living things over time

extinct when a particular type of plant or animal no longer exists

fossil fuel fuel, such as coal or oil, that has formed from the ancient remains of plants or animals

fragile easily destroyed

glacier slow-moving ice mass

global warming increase in the Earth's temperature

gulf deep ocean inlet surrounded by land

hemisphere half the Earth – the Northern Hemisphere stretches north of the equator, and the Southern Hemisphere stretches south of the equator

ice shelf thick chunk of ice that is attached to the land but sticks out into the sea

indigenous describing a person whose ancestors originate from a place; this term is often used in areas where there are also communities who can be described as colonisers or settlers

magma very hot liquid or semi-liquid rock formed deep inside the Earth

meltwater water made from melted ice or snow

migration journey an animal makes either once in its lifetime or regularly, often to breed or feed

mineral a substance formed naturally in the ground. Some can be useful, like salt, or valuable, like gold

monsoon wind which brings heavy rain, or a season of heavy rain

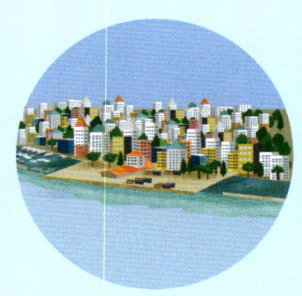

naturalist person who studies nature

navigator person who works out the direction in which to travel

oceanography science that studies the oceans

overfish catch too many of a particular type of fish

pack ice mass of thick ice, floating on the ocean

peninsula long, narrow piece of land that sticks out from the mainland, and is almost surrounded by water

plateau large area of flat, raised land

phytoplankton microscopic plants that drift in the ocean

pollution the presence of harmful or poisonous substances in the environment

resources materials, such as mineral or oil, that can be processed and used

sea large area of salty water that is part of an ocean

slavery when a person is owned by another and is made to work for them without being paid

strait narrow passage of water

subduction zone place where two tectonic plates are moving towards each other and one is pushed under the other

submersible vehicle that works underwater

tectonic plate section of the Earth's crust (rocky, outer layer)

trade buy and sell goods and services

trench deep, valley-like gash in the sea bed

tsunami huge wave, or series of waves, caused by an undersea earthquake or volcanic eruption

uninhabitable a place is uninhabitable when its conditions mean nobody can live there

venomous able to give a poisonous bite or sting

water cycle the never-ending process of water evaporating, forming clouds and falling back down to Earth in the form of rain, snow, sleet or hail

whaling hunting and killing whales

zooplankton tiny animals that float in the ocean water

Index

abyssal plains 11
Amazon river 8
Amundsen, Roald 33
Antarctica 5, 10-11, 14-15, 24-25, 36-37, 44-45, 58-59
atolls 23
autonomous underwater gliders (AUG) 35, 37
Azores 9, 19

Baltic Sea 9
basins 6-7, 10-11
beluga whales 38
Bering Strait 6-7, 12-13
bioluminescence 41

calving (ice) 25
Challenger 35
coelacanths 47
colonisation 28, 30, 35
Columbus, Christopher 28
Congo river 8-9
Cook, James 30
coral reefs 20-21, 23, 46
currents (ocean) 5, 14, 16-17, 24-25, 34-35, 52

Darwin, Charles 31
dhows 34
dolphins 9, 52
Drake Passage 14
dugongs 47, 52

eelgrass 43
equator 7, 12-13, 16-17, 26
equinox 27

fishing 50, 52
fossil fuels 51-53, 57

Gama, Vasco da 35
glacier 25, 53-54, 58
global warming 33, 53-54, 56, 58

Great Barrier Reef 20-21
greenhouse gases 53
Gulf Stream 17
gyres 17

Halley VI Research Station 36
Henson, Matthew 33
He, Zheng 34
HMS *Beagle* 31
HMS *Challenger* 29, 31
Hulhumale 53
hurricanes 16-17

icebergs 25
Iceland 6, 9, 18, 28, 32
ice shelfs 14-15, 25, 36
indigenous peoples 28, 32, 56-57
International Date Line (IDL) 12-13
Inuit 33, 56
island arcs 19, 22

kelp 42-43

manta rays 46
Mediterranean Sea 9
Melanesia 22
Micronesia 22
Mid-Atlantic Ridge 8-9, 18-19, 29
Mid-Indian Ocean Ridge 10-11
midnight Sun 27
migrations 40, 48-49
Mississippi river 8

Nansen, Fridtjof 33
narwhals 39
Northern Sea Route 6-7
North Pole 6-7, 27, 32-33
Northwest Passage 6-7

oil (crude) 51-52, 57
orcas 45
otters (sea) 43
overfishing 52

pack ice 6, 24, 39
Pangaea 5
Panthalassa 5
Peary, Robert 33
penguins 44-45
phytoplankton 42, 46
pollution 52, 54, 57
Polynesia 22
Polynesians 30

Remotely Operated Vehicles (ROV) 36
research 33, 36-37
Rhine river 8-9
ridges (ocean) 6-11, 18-19, 29
Ross Ice Shelf 14-15, 25

salmon 40
seagrass 43, 48
sea lions 43
seals 9, 39, 43, 45, 55
seamounts 10-11
slavery 29
South Pole 12, 14-15
subduction zones 19, 22
submersibles 14, 35, 37

tectonic plates 10-11
tourism 51
trades (wind) 16
trenches (ocean) 10-11, 14-15
Triangular Trade 28-29
turtles 9, 41, 48-49, 52

Vikings 28, 32
volcanoes 10, 18-19, 22-23, 35

walruses 38
water cycle 5
westerlies (wind) 16
whales 9, 38, 40, 52, 59

zooplankton 46

First published in Great Britain in 2025
by Wayland
Copyright © Hodder and Stoughton 2025

All rights reserved
Printed and bound in Dubai

Editors: Julia Bird; Julia Adams
Design: Peter Clayman
Illustrations: Josy Bloggs

HB ISBN 978 1 5263 2301 9
PB ISBN 978 1 5263 2302 6

Wayland, an imprint of
Hachette Children's Group
Part of Hodder and Stoughton
Carmelite House
50 Victoria Embankment
London EC4Y 0DZ

An Hachette UK Company
www.hachette.co.uk
www.hachettechildrens.co.uk

The authorised representative in the EEA is Hachette Ireland, 8 Castlecourt Centre, Dublin 15, D15 XTP3, Ireland (email: info@hbgi.ie)